September Revisited

A Play

Enid Coles

A Samuel French Acting Edition

SAMUEL FRENCH

FOUNDED 1830

SAMUELFRENCH-LONDON.CO.UK
SAMUELFRENCH.COM

ISBN 978-0-573-13310-7

www.samuelfrench-london.co.uk

www.samuelfrench.com

FOR AMATEUR PRODUCTION ENQUIRIES

UNITED KINGDOM AND WORLD
EXCLUDING NORTH AMERICA
plays@SamuelFrench-London.co.uk
020 7255 4302/01

Each title is subject to availability from Samuel French,

depending upon country of performance.

CHARACTERS

Carlene/Rosie
The Woman
Val/Young Nanny
Nanny

Plus optional extras

The action of the play takes place in a London park
and a nursery in Scotland

Time - the present and forty years ago

Other plays by Enid Coles:

Just A Little Word
Little Benjamin
Once and for All
Under the Twelfth Sign

SEPTEMBER REVISITED

A London Park. The present day

Two park benches, apart, are in line but very slightly angled towards the back of the stage, making one very slightly upstage of the other. The "path" they border enters by the downstage bench, continues in front of the other then turns and exits upstage, diagonally opposite its point of entry. Between the benches is a full and overflowing rubbish bin

The sound of children playing, off, from the direction of the upstage bench

The Woman sits in the centre of the downstage bench. She is bundled in many layers and has three large bulging plastic bags. She is enjoying the sunshine, face slightly raised, eyes closed. Occasionally she sways a little, happily mumbling to herself

Carlene sits with her legs up on the upstage bench. She is an untidy young woman, wearing a tatty blouse and fairly long black skirt. She is absorbed in a dog-eared cheap magazine

This opening picture is held to establish the scene

Optionally, extras can cross here and later where marked

The sound of the children fades out

Carlene (*slinging down the magazine*) Well, blow me down. I don't think much of that. (*Over her shoulder, raising her voice*) I said I don't think much of that.
Woman I heard you.
Carlene It's no sort of finish, that isn't. I thought it'd be that other feller. Him with the yacht and a pad on the Costa del Sol. I mean ter say ...

Woman There you are, you see.

Carlene It's no sort of a finish. (*She swings down her legs and stands. Calling stridently to the children*) Gary! Steve! Yes, and you, Jimmy!

The Woman winces and opens her eyes

You leave our Kimberly alone! No, I don't care what she did. She's littler than what you are. Leave her be, else I'll tan all your backsides.

Woman That's the ticket.

Carlene You've got to keep on top else they will be. (*Calling*) No, Kimberly, it's no use running to me. Clear off and play with the lads. (*She listens*) Well, bash them back! (*To The Woman*) Kids!

Woman They're never all yours!

Carlene Buzz off! (*To The Woman*) 'Course they're mine. Want to make something of it?

Woman I only asked.

Carlene *And* two at school.

Woman Lumme!

Carlene (*with a vague look towards the children*) Least, sort of ...

Woman Come on, don't you know if they're yours or not?

Carlene Well, Jimmy - he's the big one - he's my sister's kid really. I just have him, like. She only went and got herself a job, didn't she?

Woman A job? Oh, lor'!

Carlene She's a jammy beggar. It's full-time.

Woman Full-time? Oh, *lor'*!

Carlene You wouldn't say that if you knew how much she gets, like.

Woman So you have - Jimmy. Nice for you, I bet. (*She scratches her palm*)

Carlene Look, wotcher getting at?

Woman A few quid from your sister when she gets paid, eh?

Carlene Hold it, you from the Social Whatsits?

Woman Now do I look like I'm from the ruddy Social Whatsits?

Carlene They're dead cunning, that lot. Maybe they get dressed up, like.

Woman They'd have to be dead cunning, dressed in all this, a day like today. Dead cunning or cuckoo!

Carlene What the hell do you for?

Woman Language! .. May bags is full up. That's what for. And don't you come that voice with me, young woman!

Carlene Sorry, I'm sure, but -

Woman We'll say no more.

Carlene - but I get a bit jumpy when folks start ferreting about. Don't want to lose what bit of help they do give me.

Woman Oh, give you a bit of help, do they?

Carlene You're ferreting about!

Woman Oh, for crying out loud ...

Carlene OK, OK, keep your tammy on. (*She sits*) Well, they did manage to put me and the kids in - you know - B & B. Private Hotel, they call it, Hah!

Woman You're all set, then.

Carlene You think? It's nothing but a flippin' rabbit warren. We're packed in there like .. (*She shrugs*)

Woman Rabbits? (*Referring to the children*) Yes. Yes, I can see what you mean.

Carlene And shoved out straight after breakfast. Traipsing about. It's a long day, I'll tell you that much.

Woman I had noticed. The nights don't exactly whiz past, neither.

A tiny pause

She's coming again, that little lass of yours.

Carlene Go on, Kimberly, I'm busy. I don't want you.

Woman Bless her little socks.

Carlene Which socks are these, then?

Woman Eh? Oh, well, they don't want socks this weather, do they?

Carlene Let's just hope it goes on and on, then.

Woman Bless her.
Carlene You've done that bit, once. You like kids?
Woman Sort of.
Carlene Got grandchildren?
Woman (*cheerfully*) I ain't got nobody. Nor nothing. 'Cepting these. (*She pats one of the bags*)
Carlene I'm sorry.
Woman You what?
Carlene I'm really sorry.
Woman You keep it to yourself, then. It's beautiful.
Carlene You've got to be joking!
Woman Beautiful, I said. No rent, no gas meter. Thundering well beautiful!
Carlene I'll believe you, thousands wouldn't.

Val enters downstage. She wears jeans and T-shirt and her whole appearance is tidier than Carlene's

Val (*to The Woman*) Lovely day.
Woman Not too bad at all.
Carlene Oh, hi, Val. I was just beginning to wonder.
Val 'Allo, there. How's it going?

Val props herself on the back of Carlene's bench

Carlene The kids are a pain, aren't they? So what's new? Come and park your bottom. If they spy you, that's the end of peace and quiet.
Val Why don't I just go and- ?
Carlene They're all right! Come and talk to me. I've been waiting.

Val sits with Carlene

Val Washed my hair, didn't I?
Carlene It looks really good. I must have a go at mine some time. (*She sighs*) There's always something.
Val (*with a nod towards the other bench*) Where's Lady Gasbag got to, this morning?
Carlene (*with her vague look*) Oh, she's not here yet, is she?

Val Doesn't look much like it.

Carlene Funny, she's always here by the time we are.

Val Hope nothing's happened to the poor old thing.

Carlene She's got a few years to go yet.

Val Not that sort of "happened". Got roughened up or something.

Carlene It'd be a brave feller that'd rough her up.

Val Yah. I bet she's really handy with that brolly of hers.

Carlene She won't be over-happy when she does come. That's her parking place, like this is ours.

Val Could be some fun.

Carlene She'll see her off.

Val But who'll see which off, Carlene?

Woman There's room enough for the two of us.

Carlene Not for you two, there's not. Not you and Lady Gasbag. No way!

Woman Oh, ta very much.

Carlene I only meant she likes to choose her company for her bit of swank.

Val But have you noticed how the company skedaddles once she gets started? (*In imitation of Nanny*) "Glorious weather isn't it? September days have a very special quality, I always think."

Carlene That's spot-on Val. You oughter get on the box. Really, you did.

Val I might just have a go one of these days.

Carlene Do some more.

Val "We always went to Scotland in September. For the shooting, of course. We took the entire household. Well, we left a skeleton staff in London, naturally."

Carlene Oh, naturally! Cor, fancy having a dekko at the area window and seeing the skeletons all jangling about, like.

Carlene giggles until she chokes. Val slaps her on the back

Ow, steady on!

Woman Oh yes, I've come across that one, all right. But she's no lady.

Val 'Course she's not.

Carlene That was just our bit of soft. Val got it out of her. She was only the nanny.

Val All that gas about *we* did this and *we* did that. And only the nanny! And now she's just like the rest of us. Glad to find a place to park her bones.

Carlene (*set off again*) Bones!

Val Sorry I spoke.

Woman I dunno so much about "only" a nanny. Some nannies have got a lot of clout.

Val Like Jeremy's nanny.

Carlene Oy oy! Who's Jeremy, then?

Val In a book.

Carlene Aw ... only a book.

Val Jeremy called his nanny "Jampot".

Carlene Go on, then, surprise me.

Val She was jampot shape, wasn't she?

Carlene This nanny's not a jampot. More like a bottle. A vinegar bottle, at that.

Woman Poor old thing, I feel right sorry for her.

Val Well, now I've heard it all.

Woman Got something on her mind, poor blighter.

Val You think?

Woman I'm certain. Festering, it is. Eating into her.

Carlene Aagh! Do you mind?

Woman It's remorse, that's what it is.

Carlene (*standing and crossing to The Woman*) Remorse? What's that when it's at home?

Woman Being sorry about something. Something so deep it won't go away.

Carlene Look, maybe she was in with this gang, like. And they - you know - kidnapped one of the little kids she was looking after. What say to that?

Val (*referring to Carlene's magazine*) I'd say you'd been reading too many of those. That's what I'd say.

Carlene Beats me how you know all about that festering stuff, like.

Woman I listen, don't I? I've got all the time in the world to listen.

Carlene I call that really shabby. Flapping your ears at what folks are saying.

Woman 'Tisn't always what they're saying. It's what they're meaning.

Carlene Same difference.

Woman Not by a long chalk, it's not. You can take it from me, it's all to do with that Rosie she's always on about.

Val (*in imitation*) "My little nursery maid from when I was with Sir Joseph and her Ladyship."

Woman S'right.

Carlene She thought the world of Rosie. She said.

Woman Gerraway.

Carlene Excuse me, but she did. Who you calling a fibber?

Woman Hold your horses. She said it all right, granted. But she didn't think the world of her.

Carlene She had me fooled. She's always on about Rosie this, that and the other.

Woman Well, you can take it from me. I know!

Val (*looking towards the children*) Your little Kimberly looks in trouble.

Carlene As per usual. (*Turning and looking vaguely*) What's she up to now?

Val Hopping about fit to bust. Ah, maybe that's what it is.

Carlene Silly little monkey. Always leaves it to the last minute.

Val You going to her, then?

Carlene She's got to learn.

Val Look, don't you bother-

Carlene I'm not. It's her own fault if she doesn't get them down in time.

Val exits to the children

Carlene Always rushing about after them. She makes me really tired. (*She sits on the upstage bench*)

Woman She your sister, then?

Carlene Nah. My sister's got a job. I did say.

Woman So you did. Full-time!

Carlene Me and Val was at school together. Well, just about. She was a prefect when I was in the bottom class. I thought the world of her.

Woman There's always one like that when you're in the bottom class.

Carlene Ever so bright, she was.

Woman Fancy that.

Carlene Got all the prizes and that, like.

Woman And you've kept good mates all along?

Carlene Nah. Bumped into each other here, didn't we? Not so long ago. Now we meet up most mornings. Ever so good, she is, to me and the kids. She's cracked about kids.

Woman She married or something?

Carlene Not even something. Never seems to bother about fellers. I can't understand her.

Woman I can. Like you said, she's bright!

Carlene And then some. She can run rings round folks when it comes to words. You heard her about that book. She's always stuck in the library.

Woman And now can't get a job.

Carlene Who said she can't get a job? She's got a job all right. A brilliant job.

Woman But gets her mornings, seemingly.

Carlene S'right. Works second shift in a fast food place.

Woman It's a funny old world.

Nanny enters downstage and stands by the Woman's bench, glaring. She is neatly dressed and carries an umbrella. She has a rather grand accent that slips on occasions

Grinning cheerfully, the Woman moves a bag from the bench to make room. Nanny continues to glare. The Woman edges along the bench, making more room. Nanny doesn't move. The Woman's grin disappears. She stands and begins to gather together her bags. Nanny pokes at one with her umbrella, spiking the plastic

Now look what you've been and gone and done.

There is no response. Nanny seats herself in the middle of the bench

Well, you could say "sorry", then.

There is no response. Nanny looks firmly ahead

Couldn't you just say "sorry"?

There is no response

Booh!

Nanny jumps in surprise but gives no other response

Well I never! There was me thinking you was deaf.

Carlene moves along her bench

Carlene You come and sit with me. It's nicer here.

Muttering a little, the Woman moves two of her bags towards Carlene's bench

(*Standing*) OK, I'll get it.

Carlene fetches the third bag. The Woman picks up the magazine and opens it

You found that one that finishes so funny? I never dreamed it'd finish like that. I thought it'd be that other feller. Him with the yacht and a pad on the Costa del Sol. I'd have had him like a shot!

Woman Well, it was you that said it, gal! (*She closes the magazine and tucks it into a bag, then she starts to pick up her bags*)

Carlene Oh no, you don't. (*She grabs the magazine*) I've got to give that back tonight else I'll get done. You can have a bit of a read here, can't you?

Woman I'd best be pushing off. I've got a lot to see to.
Carlene Tarrah, then, see yah.

The Woman picks up the last of the bags

Woman I wouldn't be at all surprised.

With a last glare towards Nanny The Woman trudges off upstage

Carlene It wouldn't have cost you nothing to say "sorry" to her.
Nanny It was an accident, pure and simple.
Carlene You say sorry for an accident.
Nanny I don't. Not to people like that.
Carlene She's still people. (*She sits*)

A brief pause during which optional extras can pass by if desired

Nanny Has the lady with the little white dog gone past yet, by any chance?
Carlene (*shrugging*) Wasn't looking, was I?
Nanny The lady that- (*She corrects herself*) The lady who was sitting here yesterday. Sitting talking. Talking to me.
Carlene All right, all right, I've got you. (*She stands and looks each way*) No sign of her. (*She looks down and round*) No sign of the little dog, neither. You know ... (*grumbling lazily*) It's not right. Not where there's kids playing, it's not.
Nanny We had such an interesting conversation, her and I. She must have got delayed. She'll be along presently, I've no doubt.
Carlene I wouldn't count on it. Maybe she's gone a different way today.
Nanny Oh, no. We arranged to meet here again.
Carlene *You* did. *You* arranged to meet here. I didn't hear her say nothing about it, like.
Nanny Well, maybe you weren't listening in, were you?

Val enters from seeing to the children

Val Oh, 'morning. Lovely day.

Nanny Glorious weather, isn't it? September days have a very special quality, I always think. We always went to Scotland for September. For the shooting, of course.
Val (*interrupting her*) Yes, I seem to remember you saying. (*To Carlene*) Caught her, just in time. She was desperate, poor little thing.
Carlene No need for all that fuss and bother.
Val No bother. No fuss, come to that.
Carlene Running about, she'd have dried off in no time.
Val I like looking after kids.
Carlene Well, get some of your own to look after. (*She sits*)
Val I'd be good at it. I know I would.
Carlene Getting kids? I should hope so. Easiest thing in the world, getting kids.
Val The voice of the expert .. I was meaning looking after them professionally.
Carlene Yer what?
Val Being a nanny. With all these women going back to work -
Carlene Like my sister.
Val Not quite like your sister. What they call high-flyers. Phones in their cars. Briefcases. That sort of thing.
Carlene Oh, *them!* .. No, I've never come across none of them.
Val They all want nannies.
Carlene But you said you'd have a go to get on the box. I was looking forward to my friend on the box.
Val Just a joke, Carlene. Not much chance of that.
Nanny About as much chance as you becoming a nanny.
Val I beg yours?
Nanny Nannies have got to be trained, you know. they don't just happen. They have to go to one of them - (*correcting herself*) to one of those special training colleges.
Val (*moving to Nanny*) Did you, then?
Nanny There's a lot to it, I can tell you. It's not just pushing a pram round the park.
Val Did you go to one of the (*slightest emphasis*) - them - special training colleges?

Nanny Of course, there is another way. By going as a nursery maid under a good nanny. Learning that way.

Carlene Sort of apprentice, like.

Val I get it. Her doing all the work while nanny reads the kids their stories. Big deal! (*She returns to Carlene's bench and sits*)

Nanny Not at all. In superior households like ours, nursery maids had a very good time. Everything found. Good plain food. They were lucky girls.

Carlene Like that Rosie you said about? Wasn't she your nursery maid?

Nanny Did I happen to mention Rosie?

Carlene Just now and again, like. (*She nudges Val*)

Nanny Goodness, I'd completely forgotten Rosie .. I was very fond of that girl.

Val So we were given to understand.

Nanny I did my very best for Rosie. Gave her an excellent training.

Val So what happened to her?

Nanny What on earth do you mean by "happened to her"?

Val Well, did she shape into a proper nanny as well? In one of your "superior households"?

Nanny I don't know. She - well, she left us very suddenly .. I've no idea what happened to her.

Carlene What a shame. When you'd done all that for her. People!

Nanny It's you, actually, that brings her into mind.

Carlene Me?

Nanny Yes, you! Rosie was very much like you.

Carlene You don't say.

Nanny I was under the impression that I had said. Very much like you. Talk about dragged through a hedge backwards!

Carlene Oh, charming.

Nanny I had to keep on at her the whole time. Come to think of it, you two are like Rosie and I all over again.

Val You're not saying I'm like you were, then?

Nanny Indeed I am. You're very much like I was.

Val Crikey, I'll have to watch it.

Nanny Oh dear, everything has changed so much since those days. Sir Joseph has passed away. And her Ladyship. But then, she was so delicate. Now Master Dominic has succeeded.

Carlene What at?

Nanny To the title, of course. And now with three sons of his own growing up. A boy each time, wasn't that splendid?

Val Well, bully for Dominic and Mrs Dom.

Nanny Sir Dominic and her Ladyship, if you don't mind.

Carlene What's so good about a son each time? My little Kimberly's just as good as the lads.

Nanny But she can't succeed to a title.

Carlene No. No, you're right there. But come to that, I don't remember Kimberly's dad having a title, like.

Val I suppose they still come in to see you every day.

Nanny That would be difficult. They live in Scotland all the time now. They gave up the London house.

Val Money troubles?

Nanny (*lying*) Gracious, how should I know? I don't pry into other people's affairs.

Val But I thought retired nannies stayed on with the family.

Nanny I suppose that sometimes they do -

Val You didn't, then?

Nanny - and sometimes they don't. It depends on the circumstances.

Val But you didn't?

Nanny No.

Val What a shame. I like the idea of that. Dear old nanny, staying on to do the sewing and suchlike. All the family, going up to talk to her in her little room. Like Brideshead.

Carlene Not another of your flipping books, like?

Nanny (*venting her annoyance with Val*) *Must* you finish every sentence with "like"?

Carlene D'you mind?

Val Hold it, she doesn't.

Nanny Very nearly. Unfortunately, it seems to have become common usage.

Carlene Look, who you calling common?

Val stands and crosses to Nanny

Val Watch it, you're not trying to upset my chum, are you?

Nanny I wasn't using the word in that sense. I wouldn't call anybody common. Nannies from superior households use the word "vulgar". It's common to say "common".

Val You mean it's vulgar.

Nanny That is just what I said.

Val No, you said "it's common to say common". You meant "it's vulgar to say common". That's what nannies from superior households would say.

Carlene She can run rings round folks when it comes to words.

Val Come on, Carlene, I've had enough. What say I buy us some grub?

Carlene Oh, yes. Chips!

Val Not again! Can't we just have a change? How about getting some bread rolls and packets of cheese slices? Some apples.

Carlene The kids like chips ... I like chips.

Val You must have your chips, then. Come on. (*She turns to exit. Casually, over her shoulder*) 'Bye.

Val exits upstage

Carlene stands, picking up her magazine

Nanny (*standing*) If by any chance you see the lady with the little white dog ...

Carlene Yes? What?

Nanny No, it doesn't matter.

Carlene I'll tell her you're waiting for her, like.

Nanny On no account. It is of no importance whatsoever.

Carlene OK, then. (*Stridently to the children*) Come on, you lot, chips!

Carlene exits upstage

Optional extras can cross here

Nanny sits, engrossed in her thoughts

The Woman enters upstage and crosses behind the benches

Putting down her bags, she picks up something small from the ground. She spits on it, rubs it on her sleeve and, delighted, pockets it. She then rakes through the rubbish bin. Finding a Coke tin, she shakes it and hearing that it is not quite empty, drinks it off

She picks up her bags and exits downstage

Nanny I'll have to find myself another place to sit. That Carlene, she always starts me thinking about Rosie. Eh dear, if only I knew what happened to her ...

There is a lighting change

Val, wearing a masculine dressing-gown and slippers, enters as Young Nanny. She has a tartan rug which she places over the upstage bench and then sits

Carlene enters tiptoeing, as Rosie. She wears a cardigan over her clothes of the previous scene and she carries her shoes

Young Nanny Oh yes, Rosie.

Rosie's shoes fall with a thud

Rosie Ooh, Nanny! ... Ooh, you didn't half make me jump.
Young Nanny Good. (*She stands*) And what time do you call this?
Rosie Getting a bit late, is it?
Young Nanny It isn't "getting", it's "got". And it isn't "a bit", it's "a lot".
Rosie She was a poet but didn't know it.
Young Nanny Very funny. And the time is?
Rosie Well, it struck half-past as I was coming upstairs.
Young Nanny Coming? Creeping, do you mean? Thinking I was in bed and asleep long since. Half-past what?

Rosie Ten?
Young Nanny Don't be silly.
Rosie Eleven?

Young Nanny shakes her head

Oh, love a duck!
Young Nanny Exactly. So where have you been?
Rosie I've only been-
Young Nanny And no more fancy stories about being in the
    kitchen with Mary, because I checked.
Rosie Spied, you mean.
Young Nanny Checked, I said. Only my duty. I'm in charge of
    this nursery. And the nursery maid. And I'm waiting to hear
    where you've been.

A slight pause

I'm still waiting.
Rosie I went for a walk, if you must know.
Young Nanny Then why didn't you ask me if you could go for
    a walk.
Rosie Because you'd have said "no".
Young Nanny You're dead right, I would.
Rosie Well, then ...
Young Nanny It must have been some walk to last 'til this time
    of night - this time of morning!
Rosie I like walking in the dark. And it's been lovely out.
Young Nanny Apart from that heavy shower we had. (*She lifts
    her hand towards Rosie's shoulder*)
Rosie Don't you hit me!
Young Nanny I wasn't going to hit you. Hold still.
Rosie Well, stop it, then.
Young Nanny I was just making sure that your shoulders were
    dry. You don't want to catch cold, do you?
Rosie Sheltered, didn't I, while that shower was on.

Young Nanny moves behind Rosie

What you up to now?

Young Nanny Just taking the bits of hay off your back, Rosie.

Rosie And what's that supposed to mean?

Young Nanny How should I know? I can't think it means you've been in the hayloft. (*She turns away to put the pieces of hay on the bench*)

Rosie Only sheltering. Like I said.

Young Nanny (*turning back*) Just what sort of mug do you take me for?

Rosie You know, I can't think up an answer to that one, Nanny.

Young Nanny That'll do, thank you very much. You can cut out the cheek, it won't help one little bit. Now, who was he?

Rosie I beg yours?

Young Nanny You haven't been by yourself all this time. So don't try it on.

Rosie gives a huge, open-mouthed yawn

And put your hand in front of your mouth when you yawn.

Rosie I do wish you'd skip it and let's get to bed.

Young Nanny The sooner you tell me, the sooner you'll be in your bed.

Rosie starts another yawn, glances at Nanny and puts her fingers delicately in front of her mouth, finishing the yawn in her own good time

I shall find out, you know, then he's for the chop.

Rosie Look, he's not the sort of bloke that gets the chop, see? Can't we just leave it at that?

Young Nanny No, we can not!

Rosie Blimey, if you think I've been with the stable lad you've got another think coming. I'm choosy, I am. Only the best for Rosie ... the *very* best.

Young Nanny Just what are you saying?

Rosie You know full well what I'm saying. The best. Himself. The top brass.

Taken aback, Young Nanny can only shake the head

It's your own fault I've said it. Going on at me like that. I wouldn't have said nothing if you hadn't gone on at me. I've kept quiet up to now.

Young Nanny And what do you mean by "up to now"?

Rosie Come on, that's easy enough. Up to now.

Young Nanny This wasn't the first time, then?

Rosie 'Course it wasn't. But only while we've been in Scotland, mind. We had to watch our P's and Q's back in the Smoke ... No hayloft!

Young Nanny You - little - tart! With her Ladyship so poorly.

Rosie As per usual. If it isn't one thing wrong with her, it's another.

Young Nanny That'll do. Her Ladyship's very delicate.

Rosie Gertcha. She just puts it on. She's been no sort of wife to him. Everybody says.

Young Nanny We've got a nursery, haven't we?

Rosie With *one* little lad in it! She troubled herself to give him an heir, then turned her back on him. (*She grins*) If you see what I mean.

Young Nanny That's a common thing to say.

Rosie Well, I am common. I've never tried to be nothing else. But I can make him happy like she never has.

Young Nanny Don't be so disgusting.

Rosie It's not disgusting. It's beautiful. Thundering well beautiful. But you wouldn't know.

Young Nanny I should hope not.

Rosie Got no time for the fellers, have you? Just cracked about kids. Well, you can't have one without the other.

Young Nanny I can.

Rosie Other people's kids. Like young Dominic ...

Young Nanny *Master* Dominic.

Rosie Garn. I call him Dominic.

Young Nanny Not any more, you don't.

Rosie You what?

Young Nanny You're on your way, Rosie. I'll give you a month's wages instead of notice. Then you can scram.

Rosie Hang on. *You'll* give me? What about *them* giving me?

Young Nanny Oh, I don't think we'll trouble Sir Joseph and her Ladyship, do you? I'll give you the money and you can push off to the station. Now.

Rosie *Now*?

Young Nanny There's that early train that brings the milk.

Rosie But it's over two miles. And lonely, that road. What if I met somebody and -ooh gosh!

Young Nanny You're the one that likes walking in the dark.

Rosie sits on the bench

Rosie I'm tired.

Young Nanny And I don't wonder!

Rosie You want money for trains. A month's wages won't go far.

Young Nanny But Rosie, I'd have thought you'd have plenty of money.

Rosie Not a bean.

Young Nanny Well, you *have* played your cards badly.

Rosie You do think up some nasty things. I'm not that sort. I never asked for nothing and I never got nothing... 'cept him.

Young Nanny Then you'll just have to manage, won't you?

Rosie (*standing*) And what if I say "no"?

Young Nanny Come again?

Rosie What if I say I'm thundering well not going?

Young Nanny You can't do that.

Rosie What if I go to him now and tell him you're chucking me out? That you want me out of the way before he can do anything about it?

Young Nanny Now simmer down, Rosie. Just have a think. What *could* Sir Joseph do about you? What would you expect him to do? He'd be in a real spot, wouldn't he? Unhappy. And you like him to be happy, you said. Don't you?

There is no response

   Don't you?

Rosie I'd best clear out the way.

Young Nanny Best thing for everybody.

Rosie Sez you!

Young Nanny Now, look sharp. And don't wake Master Dominic, getting your things together.

Rosie Things! Us from children's homes don't have all that many things. All I've got I can bung in a couple of carriers. Who wants things, anyway? I'll be all right. It's you that worries me. The nasty way you go on, you won't have nobody by the time you're too old to look after kids. Then what?

Young Nanny The Family will always look after me. A little pension, security. There'll always be a home for me with them.

Rosie Don't you be too sure. You might not be on the cushy number you think you are. Sometimes things change. One of these days you might be all on your own. A lonely old woman on a park bench, going bonkers for somebody to talk to ... You might even wish you'd got me.

Rosie meets Young Nanny's hard gaze

No, maybe not. Just a thought.

Young Nanny pushes Rosie's shoe with her toe

Young Nanny Don't forget those. You'll be wanting them.

Rosie picks up the shoes

Rosie I'll be wanting them, all right. (*Slowly, she turns to go*)

Young Nanny No. No, don't go, Rosie.

Rosie stops

Look, we'll say no more about it. We'll just forget what happened. You can stay. (*with difficulty*) I - I want you to stay.

Rosie (*turning back*) Nah. It wouldn't do, would it? It wouldn't never do. Ta all the same, but I'll be pushing off.

Rosie exits upstage

Young Nanny Rosie! Rosie!

Young Nanny grabs the rug and exits after Rosie

Revert to previous lighting

In a daze, Nanny stands, looking in the direction Rosie has gone

Nanny Rosie! Rosie!

The Woman enters downstage and stands near to Nanny

Nanny, shaken, sits. After a moment, she becomes aware of The Woman. Slowly, she looks up and meets The Woman's eyes

Woman You all right, then? I thought I heard you call out.

There is a moment's hesitation then Nanny moves along the bench, indicating the space for The Woman

Nah. It wouldn't do, would it? It wouldn't never do. Ta all the same but I'll be pushing off.
Rosie *(off)* Nah. It wouldn't do, would it? It wouldn't never do. Ta all the same but I'll be pushing off.
Nanny I'm sorry. So very sorry.
Woman What about? Busting my bag with your brolly?
Nanny About everything.
Woman Oh, well, then ... (*She puts down her bags and sits. She lifts her face to the sun*)

A brief pause

Nanny Glorious weather, isn't it? September days have a very special quality, I always think. (*She continues as usual but is interrupted*)
Woman (*interrupting*) It's beautiful. Thundering well beautiful.
Nanny (*trying out the words and finding it easier than she expected*) Thundering well!

They sit companionably as

The curtain falls

FURNITURE AND PROPERTY LIST

On stage: Two park benches
One waste-bin, overflowing, including a part-
filled can of Coke
Object on ground
Dressing as desired

Offstage: Dressing-gown, slippers, tartan rug (**Val**)
Cardigan (**Carlene**)

Personal: **The Woman**: three bulging plastic bags
Carlene: magazine
Nanny:umbrella

LIGHTING PLOT

A park and one interior setting
No fittings required

To open: Bright sunshine

Cue 1   **Nanny**: " ... I knew what happened to her ... " (Page 15)
      Lights change to indicate change of time and location

Cue 2   **Young Nanny** exits after Rosie (Page 21)
      Revert to previous lighting

EFFECTS PLOT

Cue 1   To open   (Page 1)
Sound of children playing.
Fade when scene established

Printed by John Good Holbrook Ltd